Acc
4455

This book is to be returned on or before
the last date stamped below.

780
Facts at
your
fingertips

ANDREW MARVELL
SCHOOL LIBRARY
PLEASE RETURN

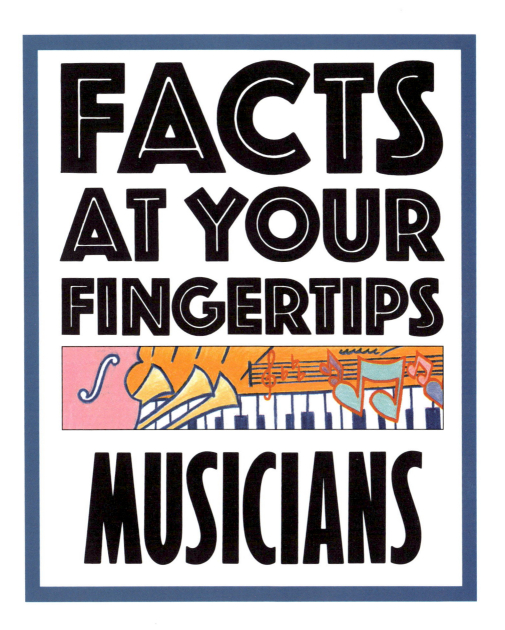

DAVID MARSHALL

SIMON & SCHUSTER
YOUNG BOOKS

This book was prepared for Simon & Schuster Young Books
by Globe Enterprises, Nantwich, Cheshire

Design and artwork: SPL Design
Photographs: ZEFA except for
Allsport (23)
The Bridgeman Art Library, London, for (6t, Bibliotheque de L'Arsenal, Paris; 19l, Forbes Magazine Collection, New York; 20, Chateau de Versailles, France/Giraudon)
BFI Stills, Posters & Designs (12t, Courtesy of Lucasfilm Ltd—™ & © Lucas film Ltd (LFL) 1977. All Rights Reserved; 12b, © 1984 Columbia Pictures Industries, Inc. © 1993 CTP Holdings, Inc. All Rights Reserved.)
Pedigree Pet Foods Ltd (22)
Redfern (7, 9, 11t, 28b)

First published in Great Britain in 1993
by Simon & Schuster Young Books

Simon & Schuster Young Books
Campus 400, Maylands Avenue
Hemel Hempstead, Herts HP2 7EZ

© 1993 Globe Enterprises

All rights reserved

Printed and bound in Belgium
by Proost International Book Production

A catalogue record for this book
is available from the British Library

CONTENTS

THE VARIETY OF MUSIC   4-17
Street music   6
Top of the pops   7
Traditional music   8
Jazz   9
Dance music   10
Marching bands   11
Film scores   12
Musicals   13
Orchestral music   14
Chamber music   15
Opera   16
Ballet   17

IDEAS EXPRESSED IN MUSIC   18-23
Telling a story   20
Describing nature   21
Describing mood   22
National pride   23

USE OF MUSIC IN DAILY LIFE   24-29
Singing   26
Playing an instrument   27
Live music   28
Recorded music   29

FACTS ABOUT MUSICIANS   30-31

INDEX   32

4

THE VARIETY

OF MUSIC

In any city, town, or village in the world, the chances are that almost immediately you will hear the sound of music. It will vary from place to place but it will certainly be music and it will belong to its own area and its own time. ▶

◀ We can never know why people first began to make music. We can only imagine that people discovered how to imitate the sounds of nature around them, and found them pleasant to their ears.

Today, we have fine instruments that are developments of instruments known for thousands of years. However, by using computer technology, it is quite possible for one musician to make the sound of a complete orchestra. ▶

STREET MUSIC

The first music was played about 40,000 years ago in Egypt using very simple instruments. It has probably always been played in the streets and performed as people go about their daily lives. Sometimes people stopped to listen just as they do today. In most towns around the world, it is probably possible to find people, at some time, playing music on the street.

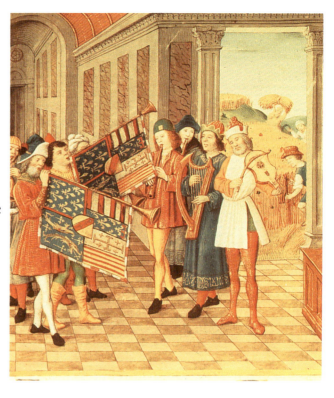

▲ In Europe about 500 years ago, bands of musicians called strolling players would travel from town to town and entertain people in exchange for food, somewhere to sleep and money.

◄ All kinds of instruments can be played in the street. Sometimes the players are poor people earning money as best they can. Sometimes they are student musicians grateful for the chance to perform.

TOP OF THE POPS

In 1954, Bill Haley and the Comets made a record called *Rock Around the Clock.* Almost overnight, pop music came into being with its own clothes, dancing and events. It was a way for young people to show they were different from their parents. Today it is an enormous business.

Michael Jackson is a very popular performer. His records sell millions of copies and many people like to go to his concerts. ▼

TRADITIONAL MUSIC

Before the invention of records, radio and television, the best way for people to enjoy music was to play it for themselves. Each place developed its own special kind of music that was handed down from generation to generation. Even today, people still like to play their traditional music.

▲ A pipe player on the high plateau in Peru, South America.

◄ Turkish musicians at an open-air concert in Germany. There are many Turkish people living in Germany who they still like to play traditional Turkish music.

Children is Scotland learn to play the bag-pipes. Scottish music has a very special sound with many well-loved songs and dances which are performed regularly. ►

JAZZ

Jazz is a kind of music that began about 100 years ago in New Orleans, a city in the southern USA. It was started mostly by black musicians who blended their traditional music with church music and other popular American music. Jazz musicians start with a basic theme which has a swinging rhythm and then make up variations as they play.

Louis Armstrong's imaginative playing helped jazz develop in the 1920s and many of his early recordings are now classics. ▼

DANCE MUSIC

Every country in the world has its own traditional dances. Dance began long ago as a part of religious ceremonies and eventually turned into the many kinds of dance existing today. The steps follow a set pattern and usually have a special meaning. Many modern dances are a way of having a good time with friends.

Dancing can be enjoyed at any time in your life. Moving to the rhythm of music is an exhilarating feeling and a good way of keeping fit. ▼

MARCHING BANDS

Marching music grew from a simple drum beat played so foot soldiers could keep in step. Bands use mainly brass instruments that are easy to play while walking along such as trombones and trumpets. They are popular at festivals especially in northern Europe and North America. In northern England, local industry or town councils pay for the upkeep of brass bands which play in competitions.

▲ The Algiers Brass Band performing at a fair in New Orleans in the USA.

◄ A flute player at the Aloha Week Parade in Honolulu, Hawaii.

FILM SCORES

The first films were silent and background music was played on a piano in the cinema. Modern films have music that is specially written for them and helps to set the mood or atmosphere of each scene. Fast and furious car chases are made more exciting by lively noisy music. Films often have tunes which are repeated at important points in the story and may be linked to the hero or heroine.

▲ *Star Wars* was a very successful space adventure that won seven awards including one for its music. The music had great pace and set a wonderful atmosphere.

(Picture courtesy of Lucas Film Ltd. ™ & © Lucas film Ltd (LFL) 1977. All Rights Reserved.)

(© 1984 Columbia Pictures Industries, Inc. © 1993 C T P Holdings, Inc. All Rights Reserved.)

◄ *Ghostbusters* was a crazy comedy about a group of people who trapped ghosts. It had a very catchy theme song that was successful as a pop song.

MUSICALS

Musicals are plays with music. They are a mixture of songs and spoken words. The songs are at important points in the story and add atmosphere to the plays. The first musical was written in the 1920s by Jerome Kern and was called *Showboat*. Successful musicals today, like *Cats* and *Starlight Express*, were written by Andrew Lloyd Webber.

A scene from *West Side Story*, a musical by Leonard Bernstein in the 1950s. *West Side Story* is about a quarrel between two poor families living in New York. Bernstein took the story from Shakespeare's play *Romeo and Juliet*. ▼

ORCHESTRAL MUSIC

Orchestras started to develop about 250 years ago because composers were writing music that needed many instruments and musicians. The music was usually long and intricate like a symphony, a ballet or an opera. Modern orchestras have four sections: strings such as violins and cellos; woodwind such as flutes and oboes; brass such as horns and trumpets; and percussion such as cymbals and drums. The musicians sit together so they give a balanced sound.

▲ Oboes are part of the woodwind section in an orchestra. They have a double reed through which the player blows.

◄ Orchestras usually play in concert halls which have been built to make the best of the sound. Open-air concerts catch the imagination and attract people who would not go to a concert hall.

CHAMBER MUSIC

Chamber music began early in the 19th century when four musicians playing string instruments gave a public performance. Chamber music became a popular way for rich people to entertain guests in their homes which is why it is called chamber music.

There are always at least two musicians but there can be as many as thirty. Small groups have all strings or all woodwind instruments but the larger groups are combinations of instruments from different families.

A string quartet playing in Covent Garden, London. ▶

OPERA

An opera is a play in which the words are sung to music. There are usually main characters and many other people who make up a chorus. A solo song is called an aria but there are also songs that involve several of the main characters. An orchestra provides the music. Performances are often grand with sumptuous costumes.

The performers of the Chinese Opera in Singapore wearing opera costume. ▼

BALLET

Ballet is a story told by music and dance. Ballet dancers are very athletic and practise for hours every day to learn the positions and movements.

Many ballets have particularly beautiful music—the dance movements are then arranged to fit the music by a person called a choreographer.

Composers of the 19th century, like Tchaikovsky, told tragic mythical stories such as *Swan Lake* and *The Sleeping Beauty*.

Maria Bylova making an amazing leap in *Spartacus*. *Spartacus* was written in 1954 by the Russian composer Khachaturian. The story tells of the triumph of good over evil in ancient Rome. ▶

18

IDEAS EXPRESSED

IN MUSIC

Composers discovered that by mixing the sounds of instruments they could make pictures in sounds. In the 18th century, composers like Mozart and Haydn wrote beautiful Classical music. ▶

◀ In the 19th century, composers reflected the disturbed and revolutionary times in which they lived. Their music was known as Romantic music.

The 20th century again brought change. People were ready to try new ideas—science, technology, music, art and design all came together to create a modern culture. ▶

TELLING A STORY

Many composers have based their music around a story—they try to arouse different feelings in you with each twist and turn of the plot. Composers create new atmospheres by using different sounding instruments and changing the speed and rhythm of the music.

Tchaikovsky based the *1812 Overture* on Napoleon's attempt to capture Moscow in 1812. The music makes you feel the frenzy of the battle and the jubilation of the people of Moscow when Napoleon retreated beaten. ▼

DESCRIBING NATURE

Nature has always been a popular theme with composers. In *The Four Seasons*, Vivaldi gives each season a completely different character, and in *The Carnival of the Animals*, Saint-Saëns describes each animal by a different instrument. In the *Pastoral Symphony*, Beethoven was able to show the many moods of nature.

Composers change the rhythms, sounds and instruments to arouse different feelings, just as a waterfall arouses different feelings from the setting sun. ▼ ▶

DESCRIBING MOOD

Deep, bass sounds cause a sombre mood, high, light sounds are happy and carefree. Some music is relaxing, other music wakes you up. People who make commercials for television use these ideas to help the commercials stick in your mind. A car advertisement may use dangerous and exciting music to stress how safe and reliable the car is. Soft, gentle music might be used for baby products to show how good they are for babies.

This is a still picture from a commercial advertising dog food. The music that goes with it is happy and carefree to show that the food makes happy, healthy dogs. ▼

NATIONAL PRIDE

Many composers have deep feelings about their countries and these show in their music. Traditional rhythms and melodies are woven into their work. Sibelius wrote a whole orchestral piece about Finland, and Smetana a collection of symphonic poems about Czechoslovakia.

Most countries have a national anthem—a piece of music played on ceremonial occasions. Anthems usually fit the culture of the country they belong to and are a show of national pride.

▲ Gwen Torrence winner of the 200 m at the Barcelona Olympics. Tears stream down her face after listening to *The Star-Spangled Banner*, the anthem of the USA.

◄ Linford Christie, leader of the British team at Barcelona, arms spread wide with joy after winning the 100 m and hearing *God Save the Queen* played in his honour.

USE OF MUSIC IN

DAILY LIFE

As you go through a day, how many times do you hear music? When you're in town is the music coming from a shop, or a band in the street? ►

◄ Do you learn an instrument? If so, perhaps you are making music for yourself.

Do you hear music on television, radio or video? Now, thanks to technology, you can carry your music with you wherever you go!

SINGING

Most people enjoy singing but some have such beautiful voices that they make singing their career. Those with the highest quality voices will sing in professional choirs or even for opera companies. Others will sing in musicals, for folk groups or to entertain huge numbers of people at concerts. In pop-singing it is not the purity of the voice that counts, but the nature of the sound they produce.

▲ Choirs have a balance of voices in different ranges. Men will be tenors, baritones, or basses, the last one being the lowest voice. Women will be sopranos, mezzo-sopranos, or contraltos, the first one being the highest voice.

◀ The Opryland Singers. Groups performing country music have a very clear style. Performers may sing and play at the same time.

PLAYING AN INSTRUMENT

In some cultures many people learn to play music, the knowledge is handed down through the family. In other countries, children are taught by music teachers. It is always worth learning a musical instrument because playing a piece of music is a pleasurable experience. To play well involves musical talent and years of dedicated practice.

Young guitar players waiting to perform at a fiesta in Santa Fe, USA, where there is a tradition of Spanish music. ▼

LIVE MUSIC

Listening to live music is quite different from listening to the radio or a cassette player. The audience are very close to the music and can show the musicians directly whether or not they liked the performance. When Stravinsky's *Rite of Spring* was first performed in 1913, its savage jerky rhythms almost made the audience riot. On the other hand, audiences at pop concerts are sometimes beside themselves in adulation.

▲ Pop concerts often have strange lighting to increase the atmosphere.

◀ In 1985, pop concerts in Britain and America were linked by satellite to raise money for famine victims in Africa. In Britain, Wembley Stadium was packed to capacity and the whole event televised around the world.

RECORDED MUSIC

In 1877, Thomas Edison invented the first machines to record and play back sound. Within a hundred years there was a huge recorded music industry worth millions of pounds. Never before had it been so easy for ordinary people to enjoy music. There are three ways of storing recorded music: on record, on cassette tape, and on compact disc. Electronic equipment ensures the recordings are of the highest quality.

The personal cassette player is perhaps the ultimate music centre. Headphones allow the listener to switch on music any place any time. ▼

FACTS ABOUT MUSICIANS

Wolfgang Amadeus Mozart (1756-1791)
Austrian composer who wrote over 600 works in his short life. A child prodigy, he toured Europe with his father and sister.
His pieces are still favourites today, especially his operas.

Ludwig van Beethoven (1770-1827)
Looked on by some as perhaps the greatest composer of all time, he was both a Classical composer and a Romantic one. He was completely deaf by the age of 45 but still managed to compose some of his greatest pieces of music.

Richard Wagner (1813-1883)
German composer who changed opera and its music. Using German legends as a basis for his work, he wrote massive scores for huge orchestras, often requiring new instruments.

Peter Ilyich Tchaikovsky (1840-1893)
Russian composer of passionate and emotional music. His ballets such as *Swan Lake* and *The Nutcracker* are favourites.

Irving Berlin (1888-1989)
Born in Russia, he lived most of his life in the USA. He wrote thousands of songs many of which are still performed. His best known musical is *Annie Get Your Gun*.

George Gershwin ((1889-1937)
Originally a jazz pianist, he became famous for his modern symphonies, like *Rhapsody in Blue*, and operas, like *Porgy and Bess*.

**Edward Kennedy Ellington
(1899-1974)**
Pianist, composer and bandleader who revolutionised big-band jazz.
He wrote hundreds of tunes including suites and film scores.
Always known as 'The Duke'.

**Louis Armstrong
(1900-1971)**
Perhaps the best-known jazz performer of all time. He played the cornet but switched to the trumpet.
His recordings in the 1920s with his *Hot Five* and *Hot Seven* made the jazz solo famous.
Known as 'Satchmo'.

**Charles Parker
(1920-1955)**
Alto saxophonist who was the main founder of modern jazz.
Many tried to copy his style.
Known as Charlie and 'Bird'.

**Benjamin Britten
(1913-1976)**
Most outstanding British composer of the 20th century. He is best known for his eight operas, his choral music and his songs. He also wrote for films and music specially for children to perform.

**Robert Zimmerman Dylan
(1941-)**
American folk singer whose early works were mainly protest songs concerned with civil rights and anti-war movements, like *Blowin' in the Wind* and *The Times They Are A'Changing*.

**John Lennon
(1940-1980)**
With fellow *Beatle,* Paul McCartney, one of the most prolific and best-known of pop-song writers.
Their song *Yesterday* is possibly the most-recorded song of all time.

INDEX

anthems 23
   God Save the Queen 23
   The Star Spangled Banner 23

ballets
   Spartacus 17
   Swan Lake 17
   The Sleeping Beauty 17

dances 8, 10, 17

film scores 12
   Ghostbusters 12
   Star Wars 12

ideas in music
   atmosphere 12, 20
   mood 12, 22
   national pride 23
   nature 21
   rhythm 10, 20, 21, 28
   story 20
instruments 5, 6, 14, 19, 20, 21, 27
   bag-pipes 8
   brass 11, 14
   cellos 14
   cymbals 14
   drums 14
   flute 11, 14
   guitar 27
   horns 14
   oboes 14
   percussion 14
   piano 12
   strings 14, 15
   trombones 11
   trumpets 11, 14
   violins 14
   woodwind 14, 15

live music 28
   bands 11, 25
   concerts 7, 8, 14, 28
   folk groups 26
   orchestra 5, 14, 16

music styles
   ballet 14, 17
   chamber music 15
   church music 9
   Classical 19
   country music 26
   film scores 12
   jazz 9
   marching music 11
   national anthems 23
   opera 14, 16
   orchestral 14
   pop 7
   Romantic 19
   symphony 14
   traditional 8, 9
musical works
   1812 Overture 20
   Pastoral Symphony 21
   Rite of Spring 28
   The Carnival of the Animals 21
   The Four Seasons 21
musicals 13, 26
   Cats 13
   Showboat 13
   Starlight Express 13
   West Side Story 13
musicians
   Armstrong 9, 31
   Beethoven 21, 30
   Berlin 30
   Bernstein 13
   Britten 31
   Dylan 31
   Ellington 31
   Gershwin 30
   Haley 7
   Hayden 19
   Jackson 7
   Kern 13
   Khachaturian 17
   Lennon 31
   Lloyd Webber 13
   Mozart 19, 30
   Parker 31
   Saint-Saëns 21
   Sibelius 23
   Smetana 23
   Stravinsky 28
   Tchaikovsky 17, 20, 30
   Vivaldi 21
   Wagner 30

radio 8, 25, 28
recorded music 29
   cassettes 28, 29
   compact disc 29
   records 7, 8, 29
   video 25

singing 26
   aria 16
   choirs 26
   chorus 16
   pop 12, 26
   solo 16
singing voices 26
songs 8
   Rock Around the Clock 7
strolling players 6

television 8, 25
television commercials 22